Papa, what is Faith?

WRITTEN BY
KAI PARK

ILLUSTRATED BY
SOFIIA LYT

Copyright © 2024 Kai Park

ISBN: 978-3-00-079517-6 (Hardback)

All rights reserved. No part of this publication may be reproduced, distributed, or transmitted in any form or by any means, including photocopying, recording, or other electronic or mechanical methods, without the prior written permission of the publisher, except in the case of brief quotations embodied in critical reviews and certain other noncommercial uses permitted by copyright law.

FOR JOSHUA & JONATHAN

On a bright sunny morning, Felix the lion is brimming with excitement. Today, he is going to climb the big hills near his house. He can't wait to see the view from the top, which he knows will be amazing. Each step is like a little adventure!

Felix and his dad begin their adventure together, both excited and ready. But little does Felix know that surprises are waiting for them.

Because very soon, they find a group of animals around something big and grey.

Felix sees it's a stone.

And there is something written on the stone: «Have Faith».

Barry the Buffalo shrugs, and Gertie the Gigantic Giraffe is quiet. No one knows. Felix's dad says, "Sometimes we have to move forward to find out."

Even Eddie the Eloquent Elephant does not have an answer. So, Felix, still curious, decides to keep going.

"Yes," his dad says calmly. "We need to cross. I'll go first, and you can follow me."

Felix gathers all his strength together. «You can do this» He tells himself as he begins to put his little toe into the big and mighty river!

Before Felix's paws can even dry, a strong wind blows in, swirling all around. Hazel the Hoopoe struggles to stay up. Felix and his dad push forward with all their might. Felix's dad says, "We're almost there! Keep going!"

The sun comes out, and the wind dies down.
Happy but tired, they keep going.

Tired and with their fur still ruffled from the wind, they finally see the mountain top. But just as they get close, someone blocks their path.

It's Swindle the Snake, looking very sneaky. "Can we pass?" Felix asks. Swindle hisses, "Follow this way," pointing off to the side. Felix and his dad wonder if they should trust her.

Swindle insists. Felix and his dad sense something's not right. Felix's dad says, "Let's trust our instincts and find another way." They quickly move around Swindle and continue through the bushes.

Even though he's still puzzled by the snake, Felix sees they're almost at the top. Excited, he takes his final steps.

At the top of the mountain, Felix looks at his dad with gleaming eyes. All the challenges seem to disappear in the joy of reaching the top. He can even spot the animals by the stone below.

What was written on that stone again?
Ah yes - have faith he remembers.
It looks like they are still wondering
what that means.

But after all these challenges Felix has his answer: Faith is a journey! And very few start. But you have to get started. Sometimes it simply means to put your little toe into the big and mighty river!

Dive deeper into the world of Felix the lion and discover more enchanting tales crafted by Kai Park.

PARK BOOKS

For more inspiring adventures and updates,
visit us at
oneparkbooks.com

www.ingramcontent.com/pod-product-compliance
Lightning Source LLC
LaVergne TN
LVHW070129100526
838202LV00016B/2252